W9-BGC-772

Hand lettering by Leslie Lee

First published 1980 by Octopus Books Limited
59 Grosvenor Street, London W1

ISBN 0 7064 1381 4

Copyright © 1980 Michael Bond

Illustrations copyright © 1980 Octopus Books Limited

Produced by Mandarin Publishers Limited,
22a Westlands Road, Quarry Bay, Hong Kong

Printed in Hong Kong

PDO 80-76

J.D. POLSON
AND THE
LIBERTY HEAD DIME

BY

MICHAEL BOND

ILLUSTRATED BY

ROGER WADE WALKER

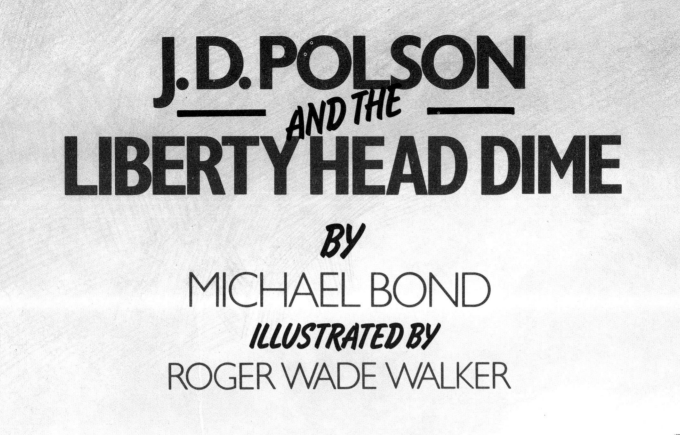

OCTOPUS

J. D. POLSON WAS BORN ON THE EAST SIDE OF A HILL IN DOWNTOWN DILLOVILLE, TEXAS, U.S.A.. IT WASN'T A GOOD START FOR ANYONE, LET ALONE AN ARMADILLO, BUT IT WAS HOME.

THEN CAME THE TIME WHEN HIS FATHER SAID TO HIM...

FEELING IN NEED OF A WASH, HE CALLED IN AT THE NEAREST
PUBLIC BATHS...

AND SUFFERED HIS FIRST SET-BACK.

IT WAS LATE WHEN HE FINALLY GOT OUT, SO HE WENT
BACK TO THE PARK, SET UP A TELESCOPE BY A BENCH NEAR
WHERE HE'D FIRST ARRIVED, OPENED UP HIS DINNER-BOX,
AND SETTLED DOWN TO TAKE HIS FIRST LONG LOOK AT
THE BIG CITY.

THE VIEW WAS MOSTLY OF BUILDINGS, CARS, AND A BIG
ROUND OBJECT WITH RED RIMS AND A BLACK CENTRE...

... WHICH TURNED OUT TO BE A POLICEMAN'S EYE.

SADDER, BUT WISER, J. D. GOT HIMSELF A FORWARDING ADDRESS AND WROTE HOME...

New York is a strange place, Mooms.

The cars all have 'Thinks Balloons' on the back (but nothing inside them)

They keep all their old things ...

... and throw away the new.

And they have park benches, but they won't let you sit on them OR eat chocolate-coated bumble bees.

Love J. D.

P.S. My Dillometer says I burrowed over 1,500 miles in three days! Is this a record?

PAN ARM

TWO WEEKS LATER A PARCEL ARRIVED CONTAINING A ROUND, BLACK OBJECT WITH A HOLE IN THE MIDDLE.

AT THE END OF THE DAY HE FOUND HE HAD TWO BUTTONS; A FRUIT MACHINE TOKEN, A TICKET FOR BLOCKING THE SIDEWALK (WHICH HE ATE) —

BE FRIENDLY TO YOUR FRIENDLY ARMADILLO

— ANOTHER TICKET FOR EATING THE TICKET HE GOT FOR BLOCKING THE SIDEWALK IN THE FIRST PLACE.....

AND A MINT CONDITION LIBERTY HEAD DIME DATED 1894 WHICH WAS A STROKE OF GOOD FORTUNE, FOR AS ANYONE WHO COLLECTS COINS AT ALL SERIOUSLY KNOWS, ONE OF THESE IS WORTH MANY THOUSANDS OF DOLLARS. IN FACT ANYONE OWNING SUCH A COIN CAN PRACTICALLY NAME HIS OWN PRICE. YOU DON'T EVEN NEED TO **PAY** FOR ANYTHING. YOU SIMPLY SHOW IT AROUND.

ONE DIME

IT WAS WHILE HE WAS SITTING ON THE SIDEWALK CLEANING HIS LEG THAT J.D. SUDDENLY CAUGHT SIGHT OF A NOTICE IN A NEARBY WINDOW....

WHILE HE WAS WAITING J. D. DECIDED TO FILL IN THE REST OF HIS FORM.

NEXT DOOR THERE SEEMED TO BE A BIG CONSTRUCTION JOB GOING ON, SO IN THE END HE GAVE UP AND WAITED UNTIL HE WAS CALLED.

NAME J. D. Polson
OCCUPATION Armadillo
ADDRESS At present I am living on a bench in Central Park but I keep getting moved on by a policeman with a night stick.
SOCIAL SECURITY NUMBER Armadillos don't have any security.
PETHATES Filling in forms like this one.

FELLOWS, I WANT YOU TO MEET J. D. POLSON. HE HAS A LIBERTY HEAD DIME IN MINT CONDITION. IT COULD BE WORTH 14,000 DOLLARS!

ARMADILLO ADVISORS

THE NEXT DAY J.D. SET TO WORK IN EARNEST. FIRST THERE WAS A GROUP PHOTOGRAPH TO BE TAKEN.

THEN THERE WERE HIS LESSONS. HE TOOK A CRASH COURSE IN HISTORY...

... LEARNED ABOUT THE NICETIES OF LIFE ...

YOU REMOVE THE BAND *BEFORE* YOU EAT THE CIGAR, J.D..

TRY HAVING ONLY *FIVE* PEAS ON YOUR KNIFE AT A TIME, J.D..

TWO PEAS?

A SPOON?

... AND THE THREE **R**'S .

AFTER THE PARTY J.D. WAS PRESENTED WITH A DIPLOMA AND BY SHOWING HIS LIBERTY HEAD DIME TO A MAN IN REAL ESTATE HE GOT HIMSELF AN OFFICE WITH A GOOD ADDRESS...THEN HE NAILED HIS DIPLOMA TO THE WALL AND SAT BACK...

AND WAITED

AND WAITED

AND WAITED

BUT HE FELT LONELIER THAN HE'D EVER BEEN BEFORE ON THE SIDEWALK.

IT'S LONELIER HERE THAN IT EVER WAS ON THE SIDEWALK.

SO HE SENT FOR HIS TEAM OF ADVISORS AGAIN ...

... AND WITH THE MONEY HE RAISED ON HIS TELESCOPE, HIS ADVISORS GAVE HIM A LIST OF VACANT BILLBOARDS TOGETHER WITH A SET OF SLOGANS...

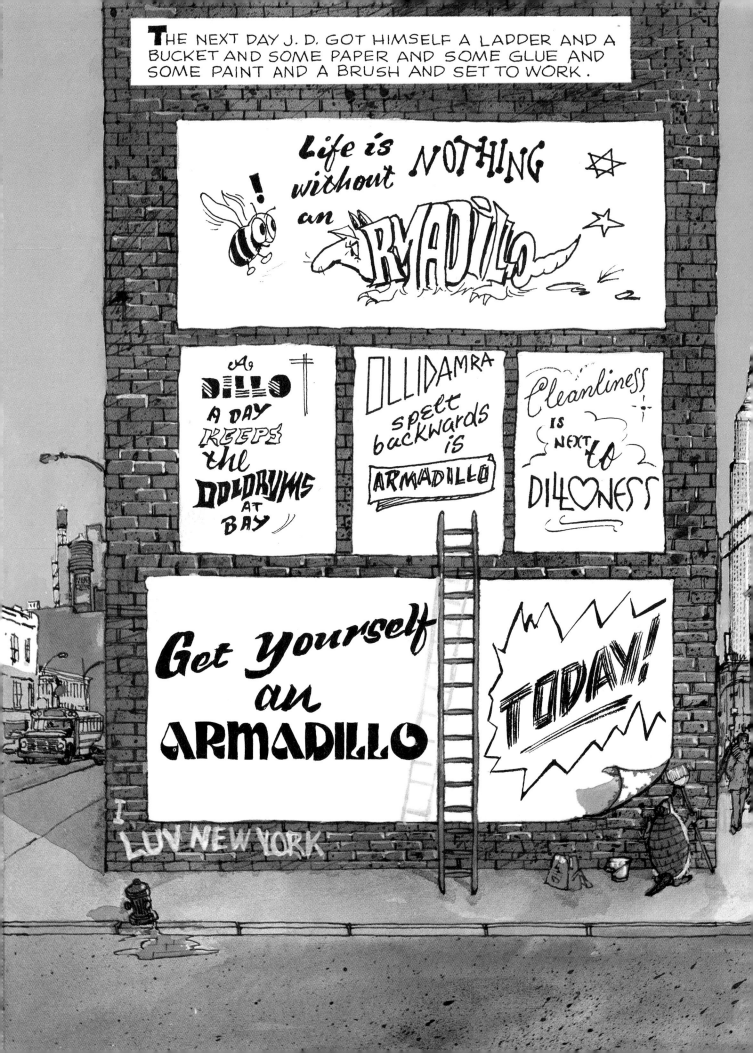

THIS TIME IT REALLY SEEMED TO WORK.
EVEN HIS ADVISORS WERE OVERWHELMED
BY THE SUCCESS OF THE CAMPAIGN....

SUDDENLY EVERYBODY WANTED HIM, AND BECAUSE HE COULDN'T BE IN A HUNDRED DIFFERENT PLACES AT ONCE, HIS ADVISORS ADVISED HIM TO HAVE CARDBOARD CUT-OUTS OF HIMSELF MADE UP...

...AND RECORDINGS DUBBED OF HIS SPEECHES.

WITH THE MONEY HE MADE...

HE PUT ON BROADWAY MUSICALS...

BOUGHT A FLEET OF TRUCKS...

... A PENTHOUSE APARTMENT JUST OFF FIFTH AVENUE...THE HIGHEST IN TOWN...AND THE BIGGEST AND MOST POWERFUL TELESCOPE HE COULD FIND.

BUT LIFE STILL HAD ITS PROBLEMS. IF HE WENT OUT HE HAD TROUBLE GETTING BACK IN AGAIN.

THERE'S AN ARMADILLO HERE. SAYS HE WANTS TO SEE J.D..

I GOT MY ORDERS. J.D. HAS TO BE PROTECTED.

BUT I *AM* J.D.!

TELL THAT TO THE MARINES!

ANYONE SEEN A MARINE?

WHERE DO I FIND A MARINE?

AND WHEN HE THREW PARTIES PEOPLE ONLY TALKED *ABOUT* HIM, NEVER TO HIM. MOSTLY THEY TALKED ABOUT HIM BEHIND HIS BACK. SOME TALKED ABOUT HIM BEHIND HIS CARDBOARD CUT-OUTS. OTHERS EVEN TALKED ABOUT HIS CARDBOARD CUT-OUTS BEHIND HIS CARDBOARD CUT-OUTS.

THEY'RE ALL CURLY AT THE EDGES!

HAVE YOU SEEN HIS CARDBOARD CUT-OUTS LATELY?

PERHAPS SOME ARMADILLOS ARE BORN LONELY...

EVEN MY CHOCOLATE-COATED BUMBLE BEES LEAVE A NASTY TASTE!

WHAT'S THAT PLACE OVER THERE—THE ONE WAY OUT BEYOND THE CITY?

THE RESULT WAS A FOREGONE CONCLUSION . . .

P.S. HOW DOES IT FEEL TO HAVE THE LONELIEST JOB IN